INSECT
FACTS
AND
FOLKLORE

iNSECT

FACTS
AND
FOLKLORE

L. PATRICIA KITE

THE MILLBROOK PRESS
Brookfield, Connecticut

To Snoofles, Blessing, Mees-Moos, and Sue-Bitty Kite,
as well as Muzzy, Pumpkin, Cecily, Cocoa, and Lucas . . .
. . . and to all the library staff who have been so kind to me
as a child and as an adult.

Cover photograph courtesy of Animals Animals (© James H. Robinson)
Photographs courtesy of Animals Animals: pp. 2-3 (© Bill Beatty), 12 (© Jack Clark), 15
(© Patti Murray), 18 (© O.S.F.), 26 (top: © Steven David Miller; bottom: © G. W. Willis), 30
(© Patti Murray), 36 (© R. F. Head), 39 (© Robert Lubeck), 41 (© Bill Beatty), 46 (© R.
Blythe/OSF), 68 (© Robert Maier); © Bill Beatty: pp. 8, 20, 33, 60, 70; © William E.
Ferguson: pp. 24, 44, 49, 52, 54; Peter Arnold, Inc.: pp. 58 (© John Cancalosi), 63 (© David
Scharf); Omni-Photo Communications: p. 65 (© Nathan Beck)

Published by The Millbrook Press, Inc.
2 Old New Milford Road
Brookfield, Connecticut 06804
www.millbrookpress.com

Library of Congress Cataloging-in-Publication Data
Kite, L. Patricia.
Insect facts and folklore / L. Patricia Kite.
p. cm.
Includes bibliographical references (p.).
ISBN 0-7613-1822-4 (lib. bdg.)
1. Insects—Juvenile literature. 2. Insects—Folklore—Juvenile literature.
[1. Insects. 2. Insects—Folklore. 3. Folklore.] I. Title.
QL467.2.K585 2001
595.7—dc21
00-050074

CONTENTS

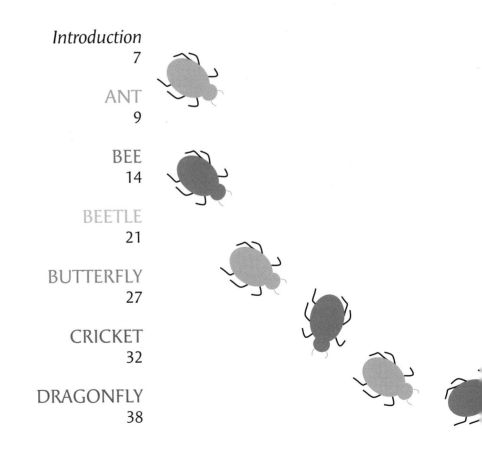

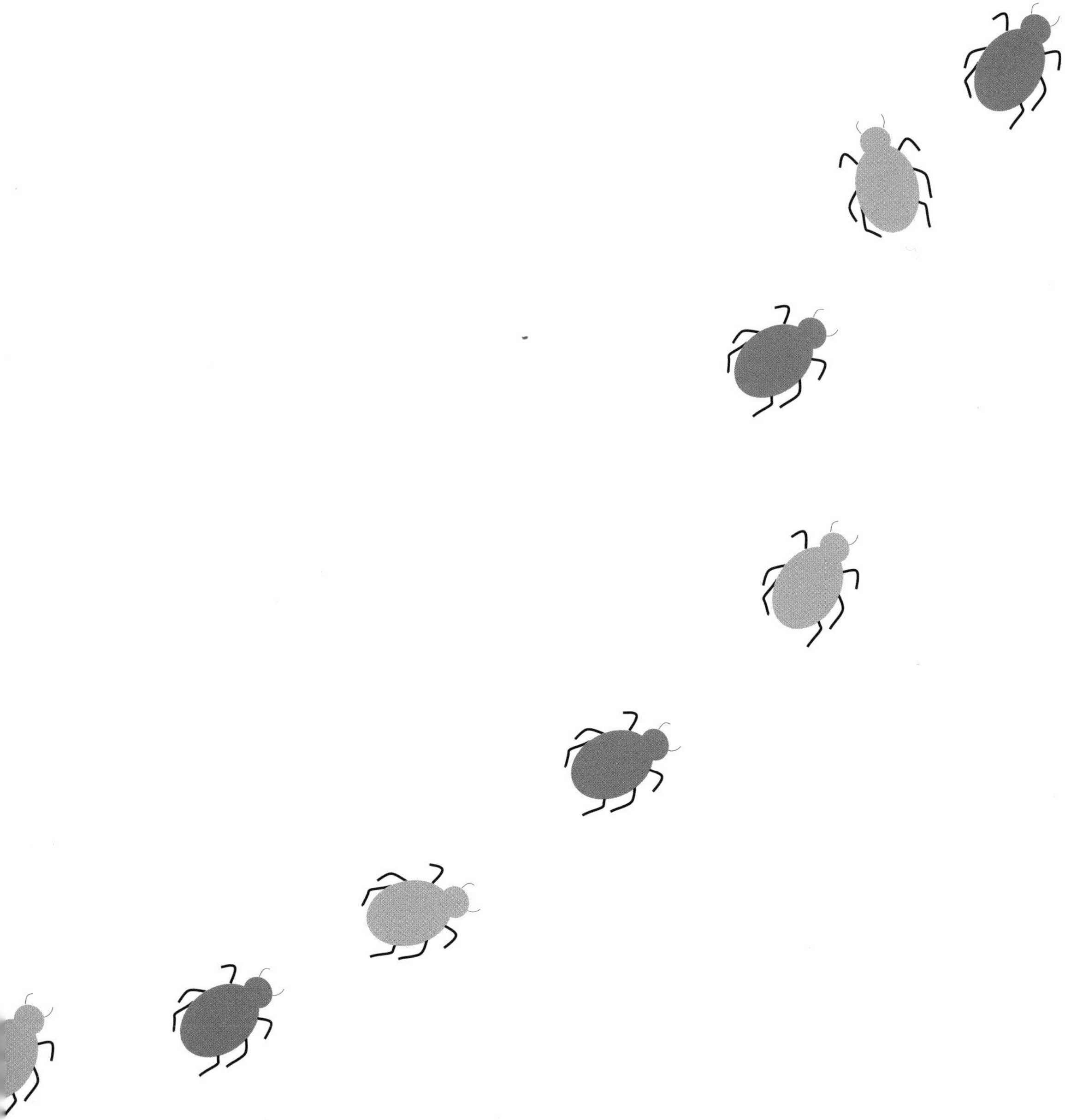

INTRODUCTION

People and insects have been co-existing since before recorded time. Just as they are today, some insects of old were pests, such as fleas and wasps. Others, including locusts and ants, threatened food supplies. Bees, on the other hand, were highly prized for their honey. Meanwhile, butterflies brought beauty to the skies, dragonflies zipped through the air, and fireflies blinked their mysterious light. In the world of long-ago, and even in many areas today, people looked to animals and insects for luck, wealth, weather forecasts, help with farming, and a way to send various messages to certain gods. Superstitions sprang up. Storytellers told "how it came to be" tales that were passed from one generation to another, often changing along the way. This book creates a bridge between the worlds of modern science and the beliefs held for so many generations, so that each insect is seen not only as a present living creature, but also one with a fascinating past history.

Little black worker ants surround the queen.

ANT

There are about 15,000 different ant *species*, perhaps more that scientists haven't discovered yet. You may see ants in your kitchen, school yard, or playground. You may even find an ant nest, where thousands of ants may live. Sometimes you see them carrying food tidbits; other times they may be carrying tiny white dots. These dots are ant eggs or young ants. The ants may be transporting these eggs, *larvae*, and *pupae* to a safer spot, or the cargo may be the young of another type of ant being brought into the nest to become servants.

One of the most common ants seen by city and suburban people is the little black ant. Shiny black or dark brown, it is one of the smallest ants, just 1/16-inch (1.6 millimeters) long. Little black ants eat just about any type of human food, including cake, cooked vegetables, and bits of meat.

Little black ants are sometimes called "house ants." But there are several other ants that find houses and apartments to be comfortable cafeterias. The reddish-brown pharaoh ant eats not only the foods you eat, but also other insects and household items such as shoe polish and kitchen sponges.

A *species* is a biological category made up, in general, of animals or plants that can interbreed and make more young.

Larvae are insect young emerging from eggs in grub, wormlike, or caterpillar form.

A *pupa* (plural pupae) is the resting stage of insect growth between the larva and the adult.

9

Other common "house" ants include the brownish Argentine ant, which just loves sweets and fruits, including fruit juices. This tiny ant, up to 1/10 inch (2.8 millimeters), may wander into a refrigerator in search of sugary things and has been seen crossing ice to get to a tasty tidbit. There are also yellowish thief ants, so tiny that you may not even notice their visits.

Some fire ants are "house" ants too, even though they don't come inside the house. They may live under rotten wood, in concrete, and under home fireplaces where heat encourages year-round breeding. These somewhat larger ants range in size from 1/16 to 1/4 inch (1.6 to 6.4 millimeters) long. Fire ants get their name because they sting and bite, the result being a very strong burning sensation, like fire. There are several types of fire ant, including the southern fire ant, which is brownish-red with a yellowish chest. These fire ants may live in nests up to 4 square feet (.4 square meters).

Depending on the species, ant nests may be above or below ground. While the habits of each of the 15,000 species do vary, in general, each nest has one queen. She is the largest ant in the nest and in some species may grow to 2 inches (5 centimeters) in length. Once she settles in and begins laying eggs, that's all she does for the rest of her life. A queen ant may lay over a hundred eggs per day.

Taking care of the queen is the job of the worker ants. The workers also build the nest, keep it clean, take care of the young, obtain food, and protect the nest from raider ants and other enemies.

Some ant nests have different types, sizes, and shapes of workers. The honey ant species includes some workers that specialize in being honey containers. During spring and summer when there is lots of food, these special ants are fed sugary substances. They hang by their claws from the ceiling of a nest room, while their *abdomens* get bigger and bigger as they are filled. In winter, and at other times when food isn't as plentiful, other ants stroke the abdomens of the honey ants with their *antennae*, and get some drops of sweet liquid in exchange.

Ants also get some sweet liquid from their "cows." Some ant species store the eggs of aphids in their nests during cold weather. Aphids are tiny *sap*-sucking insects that give off a sweet fluid as part of their waste material. When the aphids hatch, ants may carry them to greenery to feed.

In order to get more of the aphids' sweet fluid, the ants may stroke the backs of their aphids, as if they were milking a cow. Since the aphids help with the food supply for the nest, the ants take good care of them. Ants protect their aphids from ladybugs, who like to eat aphids. And some ants build little earth coverings over their aphid "cows" to protect them from rain and heat.

There are also ants that eat only meat, live or dead. These include the army ants of South America and the driver ants of Africa. These marching ants move in long columns of as many as 20 million ants, munching on whatever is in their path. People take their pets and food animals and leave when meat-eating ants start a march. The people come back to very clean houses, with all pest insects gone, eaten by the ants.

How long can an ant live? It depends on the species. One British researcher kept a female black ant for fifteen years. What's the biggest ant? Scientists debate about that. Does one count the size of the jaws? Does one count width as well as length? A worker Ponerine ant, from Brazil, can measure 1 1/3 inches (3.3 centimeters) long. But the wingless queen of a nest of South African *Dorylus helvolus* ants can reach 2 inches (5 centimeters) long.

Even though some ants can become pests in the kitchen and in agriculture, ants are considered quite helpful in nature. Their travels through the ground loosen soil so plants grow better.

The *abdomen* is the back section of the three parts of an insect's body.

Antennae are the feelers on top of an insect's head. Each insect has two antennae.

Sap is a nourishing liquid within a plant and its leaves.

Dorylus helvolus is a latin name. All species of plants and animals have latin names in addition to their common names. This helps scientists to classify and study them. Some of the insects mentioned in this book are called by their Latin names, as you will see.

Diverse cultures throughout the world believe that ants have the power to foretell the future. Native American Wiyot mythology tells how black ants became messengers with the ability to warn tribes about upcoming earthquakes. For this reason, Native Americans, according to the story, do not build their homes on the nests of ants.

In Europe, a widespread superstition insists that it is unlucky to destroy an ant nest built close to your door. A nearby nest foretells riches in your future.

From old-time North American farmers comes advice on looking for your cows. Find an anthill, then call "doodle" three times. The direction that the ants run indicates where the cows are.

Because ants are a symbol of energy in some cultures, Moroccan shamans would feed them to their patients who were sleepy all the time.

An ant feasts on an aphid's sweet meal.

THE ANT MEN

The ancient Greek god Zeus was in love with Aegina, a mortal woman. Unfortunately, Zeus had a wife, the goddess Hera. Hera was, as usual, extremely angry with her unfaithful husband. She wished to punish him. But how? As a god, he was immortal.

Hera couldn't punish her husband, but she could punish the country where the girl lived. And so Hera created a plague. This plague destroyed so many people that almost none were left.

Aeacus, the king of this country, went to the altar of Zeus. He prayed to Zeus to stop the plague and bring back to life the people it had killed. Zeus sent a lightning bolt signifying his agreement. Near the altar of Zeus there was a sacred oak tree. A trail of ants was climbing the tree. "Give me as many people as there are ants on this tree," pleaded Aeacus.

That night, King Aeacus dreamed that the ants had been turned into men. When he awoke the next morning, it was true. The ants had all changed into soldiers. These ant people were called Myrmidons, after the Greek word for ants. They were fierce soldiers, obeying every order of their leader, whether it was the right or wrong thing to do.

If you look in a dictionary today, you will find the word myrmidon. A myrmidon is a soldier who will follow commands whether they are right or wrong. You will also find the word myrmecology, which is the study of ants. Scientists who study ants are called myrmecologists.

In India, Africa, Honduras, and other parts of the world, varying species of large black biting ants were once used to heal wounds. While the sides of a gaping wound were held together, an ant was placed above the wound. The ant's jaws would bite down. Other ants would then be put in place all along the wound. Once all the ants were in place, their heads were snapped or twisted off. The ants' jaws acted like stitches, holding the edges of the wound together until it healed.

Any hustle and bustle around ant nests may predict that rain is on the way. If a storm is approaching, ants supposedly carry their young from one place to another. Partially covered ant nest entrances are also signs of coming rains. Clear entrances, on the other hand, signify clear weather.

13

BEE

Pollen is a fine, usually yellow, powdery grain produced within flowering plants.

Honey is flower nectar that has been changed by a bee's digestive system and then ripened in the hive.

There are more than 3,500 bee species in North America. They range in size from 2/25 to 1 3/5 inches (2 millimeters to 4 centimeters) long. Bee habits vary according to species. There are mining bees that live in tunnels. There are leaf-cutting bees that cut round circles out of leaves to use in lining their egg cells. There are digger bees that make their home in clay or sand. There are cuckoo bees that place their eggs in the nests of other bees.

All bees are covered with featherlike body hairs. When a bee visits a flower, *pollen* grains stick to the hair. When the bee visits another blossom of the same type, some of the pollen comes off. This pollinates the receiving plant, enabling it to produce seeds for future plants, plus perhaps edible fruit and vegetables. The females of some bee species also collect pollen in a special pollen basket or brush located on a hind leg. This pollen, rich in protein, is used to feed their young or larvae.

Of the many bee species, honeybees and bumblebees are the only ones that make and store *honey*.

A pollen-covered bumblebee does its job.

Honeybees visit over 250 different types of flowers. Females carry the pollen and *nectar* back home in their pollen baskets. Home may be a hollow tree, a deep rock crevice, or a hive kept by beekeepers. There are about 30,000 honeybees in each colony, or group of bees. Some are males, or *drones*. Most are female workers. Their jobs include getting the water out of nectar so it becomes thick, sweet honey. The workers feed honey and protein-rich pollen to the young bees and keep the hive in good condition. Workers also feed the queen. There is only one honeybee queen per bee colony.

The honeybee is not native to North America. In 1622, settlers arriving from England brought honeybees with them. But these first imported honeybees were small and bad tempered. Native Americans called them "white man's flies." By the late 1800s, honeybees that didn't sting so readily were brought from Italy and other places in Europe. These are the bees now raised by amateur and professional beekeepers.

Honeybees have a flight and body "language" to tell each other the location of good pollen and nectar blossom sources. The odor on a bee's body tells other bees what type of flower it has visited. Information about the distance and direction of the best flowers is communicated by the bee in special flight dance movements when it returns to the colony. If the flowers are closer than three hundred feet (92 meters), the bee does a circular, or round, dance. If the flowers are further than three hundred feet, the bee does a figure-eight dance with a waggle between. The speed of the waggle gives the distance to the flowers, and the angle of the waggle gives the direction.

To manufacture one pound (0.5 kilogram) of honey, bees must visit about two million flowers. Just one active commercial hive can hold 400 pounds (181 kilograms) of honey. That's over 800 million visits to flowers by bees. Today, in the United States, honeybees pollinate almost $10 billion worth of crops yearly.

TELL IT TO THE BEES

Throughout most of Europe long ago, if something important happened in a home, people had to go out right away and whisper the incident into a local beehive. "Tell the bees" was a common saying. If one forgot to do this, the bees might die, fly from the hive, or just stop making honey.

If the head of the household died, someone in the house was supposed to tie a black cloth on each of the household's hives. Wine and sweet breads might also be set out for the bees to share. It was believed that this mourning ritual prevented the bees from developing an illness or dying as their owner had. Bees in a local hive were told not only of deaths in the family, but also of births, weddings, and the start of local projects. Then, too, bees might get a treat, including a bit of wedding cake.

When early immigrants came to North America, they carried many customs with them, including "Tell the bees." How did this bee-message originate? No one is certain. But most think the beginning of "Tell the bees" came from a very early myth. This myth said that bees carried messages to the gods.

HOW THE HONEYBEE CAME TO BE

There are many ancient stories about how bees came to be. Early Egyptians believed that bees developed from the tears of the sun god. A German folktale tells that bees were created to provide wax for

In Egyptian hieroglyphic language, the sign for the bee was a sign of royalty. Honey was used to sweeten cakes and other desserts. It was also used in the making of mummies.

A honeybee stings only once. The stinger remains in an animal's skin. Why? The stinger has barbs that hold it firmly in place. In order to get away, the bee must pull away. This fatally tears its body.

The bumblebee can sting many times. How do you tell a honeybee from a bumblebee? It's not always easy. You'd have to study the veins in their wings.

What can you do to prevent bee stings? Don't wear perfume, including perfumed shampoos. Keep your shoes on. And don't walk around with open food, particularly sugary food or drink.

The bee is a symbol of the Hindu gods Krishna, Vishnu, and Indra, who are called the "nectar-born," or Madhava. These gods are often depicted resting on a lotus flower accompanied by a bee.

Honeybee workers greet one another. They may be communicating information about good places to find pollen.

church candles. A Filipino tale talks about a man who had three daughters. Only the youngest was kind to her father in his old age. So the father changed the eldest into a cicada, the second into a spider, and the youngest into a honeybee, who would always be loved.

An Australian tale tells of two ancient tribes that lived together. One tribe worked hard to save food, including honey. The other tribe was lazy. Eventually the hardworking tribe got tired of supporting the lazy one and moved away. After many, many years, the hardworking tribe somehow transformed into bees. What happened to the people in the lazy tribe? They became flies, finding food in garbage.

In ancient Greece, it was told that the bees came complaining to the great god Zeus. "We work very hard for our honey," they said, "and people keep stealing it."

"What do you want from me?" asked Zeus.

"We want to be able to kill intruders with our stings," the bees replied. "That will keep them away."

Zeus didn't like this idea at all. But he compromised. A bee could make a harmful sting, but in doing so it would lose its stinger and die itself.

In Russia, it was considered sacrilege to kill a bee. There was an ancient belief throughout parts of Europe that the souls of men and women return to earth as bees.

Superstitions surround bees. If a bee flies into your home, that means a stranger, or a visitor, will arrive soon. If a bee flies into your house, then out again, you will soon be very lucky. If a bee buzzes a sleeping child, that child will be forever lucky. But don't let a bee die in your house: that's certain bad luck. It's also bad luck if a bee stings you. But if you dream of bees, that's good luck because they are hard workers.

A scientist wanted to know how fast a honeybee could fly. It's not easy to measure an insect's flight, but the honeybee clocked at 7 miles (11 kilometers) per hour for a short distance.

19

Beetles come in many colors and patterns: black, red, blue, green, yellow, purple, orange, shiny metallic; some have spots or stripes, or hairlike fringes. In some areas of the world, including Australia, the West Indies, Mexico, New Guinea, Thailand, and India, very brightly colored and metallic beetle wings have been used as body and costume decoration.

There was some debate about the fastest runner among the many insects living on land. The finalists were the American cockroach and two species of tiger beetles from Australia. After much scientific timing and distance testing, *Cicindela eburneola*, one of the Australian tiger beetles, was deemed a champion. If compared to a human runner, with adjustments for size, this beetle can move, for short distances, at about 720 miles (about 1,160 kilometers) per hour. Unlike most other tiger beetle species, which have wings and use flight to avoid enemies, *Cicindela eburneola* doesn't have wings. It is speedy instead.

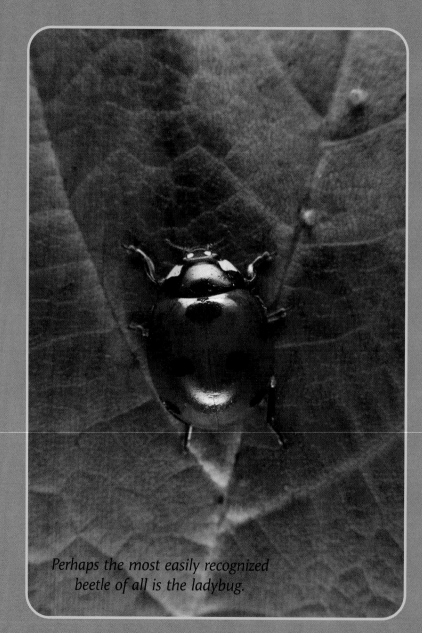

Perhaps the most easily recognized beetle of all is the ladybug.

BEETLE

There are at least 300,000 different species of beetles, with 30,000 species living in North America. Beetles make up one third of all known insects. They range in size from less than 1/16 inch (1.6 millimeters) to large tropical species that can reach 8 inches (20 centimeters) long. One of the largest North American beetles is the elephant stag beetle, which may reach 2 3/8 inches (6 centimeters) long. The gigantic jaws of the stag beetle look vicious. But the males use them only in strength contests with other males when competing for mating territories.

Beetles can live almost anyplace, depending on the species. Some live in water, such as the waterlily leaf beetle. Many others fly. Most can crawl on land. Beetles may live on a beach, floodplain, or farm, or in gardens, pastures, meadows, or forests.

Beetle diets vary. Some beetles eat only a few types of food or just one, such as the agave billbug, which eats only the sap of agave plants. Others are *predators*, such as the large diving beetle, which eats small fish, tadpoles, and insect larvae. Some, such as the American carrion

A *predator* is an animal that hunts, kills, and eats other animals.

The heaviest insect is the African goliath beetle. Adult males of this species can measure 4 3/4 inches (12 centimeters) and weigh almost 4 ounces (113 grams). These heavy beetles can still fly. African children sometimes play with them by temporarily tying a beetle to a piece of string and encouraging it to fly around in circles.

beetle, are scavengers, which feed on leftovers like dead animals and fly larvae. And there are a few that are *parasites*, such as the beetle that spends nearly its entire life living in a beaver's fur. Some beetles, such as the golden-haired flower longhorn, can be beneficial as plant pollinators. Others can be a nuisance, such as the rice billbug, which devours stored foodstuffs, such as rice.

Beetles have many different ways of defending themselves against predators. The bombardier beetle gives off a chemical liquid from its tail end that explodes with a popping sound. This becomes a stinky, irritating, cloudlike, protective screen. The gold-necked carrion beetle can roll on its back and buzz with its wings. It sounds like a bumblebee and looks a bit like one, too, so enemies are frightened off. The horned fungus beetle pretends it is dead. When still, it looks just like a piece of rotting wood. And the short-winged blister beetle not only falls over and pretends it is dead, it gives off liquid droplets from its leg joints that cause blisters on any prospective predator that doesn't take the hint to go away.

BUG VS. BEETLE

What's the difference between a bug and a beetle? They are related, since they're both insects. But bugs and beetles have differing ways of growing from egg to adult. Beetle young emerge from the egg as larvae, also called grubs. These young don't look like the parents and may have entirely different lifestyles. A beetle larva sheds its outer covering (exoskeleton), or molts, several times. After the final molt, it enters a resting period. It is now called a pupa. The entire body of the beetle changes shape until, finally, an adult beetle is formed. This process is called a complete *metamorphosis*.

Bugs emerge from eggs looking much like their parents, only smaller. The young are called nymphs. They usually eat the same food as their parents. Through a series of molts, the nymphs reach adult size. This procedure is called an incomplete metamorphosis.

There's also a quicker way to determine whether an insect is a bug or a beetle, but you must start with an adult insect. A beetle has a line down the middle of its back where the hardened front wings, or elytra, meet together in a straight line. The hindwings, used for flying, are kept folded underneath the front wings. When a flying beetle takes to the air, the elytra are held upward and out of way. In general, beetles have biting or tearing *mouthparts*, as well.

A bug has no straight line down the center of its back. Bugs also have piercing and sucking mouthparts. So the next time you see a shield bug, stink bug, milkweed bug, leaf-footed bug, lace bug, box elder bug, water strider, backswimmer, leafhopper, cicada, mealybug, or aphid, you can identify it as a bug.

WATER BEETLE CREATES THE WORLD

Once, all animals lived in a place higher than the sky. But as they multiplied, their home became very crowded. The animals could see there was a place very far down below them that was completely covered by water. The animals wondered if there might be some solid place on the water where they might live. But none of them wanted to jump down to find out.

Finally Water Beetle said it would go. Water Beetle swam for a long time, but could find no land. Unwilling to return home with news of defeat, Water Beetle decided to make land. Diving to the very bottom

In stories, particularly the scary kind, you may read of a death watch beetle. It makes a "tap, tap, tap" sound that is believed by some to foretell an upcoming death in the family. The sound has terrified people for centuries. How did this superstition come about? The death watch beetle lives within wood, including furniture, flooring, and house-support timber. During their courtship activities, females knock their heads repeatedly against the sides of their burrows, trying to attract a mate. When a house is quiet, as it usually was when a member of the houshold was gravely ill and soon to die, for example, the tapping sound may be clearly heard.

For scientists, the question sometimes is whether to count antennae or horns when measuring length. If antennae are included, a New Guinea longhorn beetle measures 10 1/2 inches (27 centimeters).

23

A beetle, like this tiger beetle, is easily identified by its hard, folded wings and the straight line down its back.

of the water, Water Beetle carried up some mud and let it float on the water's surface.

The mud began to spread out, getting wider and wider. After a while it formed an enormous island. As the mud dried, the birds came down first to test it out. Later the rest of the animals came down. Then, because it was dark on this Earth, the animals fetched the sun for light.

Variants of this tale are well known among Native American, Indian, and Asian storytellers. In a Native American tale of long ago, a beetle was given a bag of stars. Beetle, not knowing what was in the bag, was to carry it from the underworld to Earth. Curious as to what was in the bag, Beetle bit a small hole in the bag. Stars flew out and scattered across the sky.

Common names of North American beetles include beautiful tiger beetle, fiery searcher, marbled diving beetle, gold-and-brown rove beetle, big-eyed click beetle, fire beetle, and nine-spotted ladybug beetle.

To the ancient Egyptians, one species of beetle, the sacred scarab, was a symbol for Ra, a sun god. Ra arose anew each day, demonstrating rebirth and the eternal renewal of life.

The male sacred scarab beetle makes a ball of animal waste, or dung. The female inserts a single egg in the ball. The parents then roll this ball across the ground, leaving it on a sunny site. When the beetle grub hatches, it feeds on the dung.

Since only one young scarab beetle eventually emerges from each dung ball, this encouraged the Egyptian idea that the new beetle was a reincarnation of a parent beetle. The rolling of the dung ball signified the sun as it rolled across the heavens. The ancient Egyptians believed a giant scarab beetle pushed the sun as it rolled across the heavens. Scarabs, both real and made of clay, were placed in Egyptian tombs.

The swallowtail caterpillar has large false eyes on its body, which help it to ward off predators . . .

. . . And when it becomes an adult swallowtail butterfly, its bright color lets predators know that it tastes bad!

BUTTERFLY

There are at least 125,000 species worldwide of the group of insects that includes butterflies and moths. How do you tell a butterfly from a moth? Butterflies always fly during the day, whereas moths usually fly at night. Butterflies tend to be brightly colored. Moths are often plain. There are a few moths that fly during the day. These moth day-fliers tend to be brightly hued and often confused with butterflies. Butterflies usually rest with their wings upward. Moths hold their wings outward, down near their bodies, or flat against a support when at rest.

Most adult butterflies feed on flower nectar, but some feed on plant sap. Butterflies and moths are the only insects with a sucking mouthpart that looks like a long, coiled tube. This mouthpart uncoils to reach into the flower for food.

Butterflies come in many different colors and sizes. They can be orange, blue, copper, red, white, violet, brown, black, and multicolored. In North America, the smallest butterfly is the western pygmy blue with a wingspan of less than 3/8 inch (9.5 millimeters). The largest in

Blackfoot Native Americans of North America believed that the butterfly brought dreams, plus news, to people when they were sleeping. If you had a problem getting to sleep, you might be advised to watch a butterfly.

Because the butterfly changes from caterpillar to pupa to a winged creature, it has been throughout recorded history symbolic of life, death, and a magical rebirth. The belief that butterflies are souls of the dead is widespread among many cultures, including African, Asian, European, and Native South and North American. Depending on the culture, these souls of the dead might be searching for new bodies to inhabit, or they might be happy dead who come back to tell relatives that all is going well. The Australian Aborigines consider caterpillars the form in which the dead go into the afterlife before returning to Earth as spirits.

North America is the giant swallowtail, which may have a 5 1/2-inch (14-centimeter) wingspan. The butterfly with the very largest wingspan is a rare species, the Queen Alexandra's birdwing, found in Papua New Guinea. Females may have up to an 11-inch (28-centimeter) wingspan.

Butterfly young, or larvae, are called caterpillars. They don't look at all like the adult butterfly, and the young of various species often look different. Caterpillars may be smooth, such as the American copper, have spines, such as Harris' checkerspot, or be quite hairy. Caterpillars can be plain or brightly colored. A few, such as the larvae of the white tiger swallowtail, have fake eyes or other *camouflage* to confuse enemies. The harvester caterpillar creeps over to aphids, eats them, and places aphid parts in the sticky hair on its back. The larvae of some butterflies emit a stinky odor if annoyed.

Female butterflies lay their eggs on plants, often plants that the species prefers to eat. After the caterpillars emerge, most begin feeding on leaves, although the caterpillars of gossamer-winged butterflies may live in anthills, feeding on ant larvae or debris. After a specific time that varies with each caterpillar species, the butterfly caterpillar changes form. This new form is called a chrysalis, and it is usually attached to a food plant by a silk thread. Within this chrysalis, the caterpillar transforms into an adult.

Since a butterfly has many predators, it may have protective devices. The monarch butterfly and caterpillar feed only on milkweed plants. During the feeding, the insect takes in a substance that doesn't harm the insect, but makes any predator ill. Predators quickly learn to leave this orange and black butterfly alone. Not to be outdone, the viceroy butterfly has evolved coloring that mimics the monarch.

Enemies have learned that they will get sick if they eat a monarch, so they avoid the viceroy. Other butterflies with a bad taste include the green swallowtail, gulf fritillary, zebra, and queen.

THE MONARCH BUTTERFLY

In late September and early October each year, monarch butterflies begin their *migration* southward. Gathering from various sites in the United States and Canada, millions of monarchs fly up to 2,000 miles (3,200 kilometers) to their winter homes, often in central Mexico. Here they spend the winter in a state of semi-*hibernation*. Early the following spring, they start their return trip to the north, laying eggs as they go. The hatching butterflies also travel northward. These lay eggs upon arrival.

The following year, the migration southward takes place with the grandchildren, who somehow know exactly where to go over the long journey. Millions of these butterflies migrate, stopping in the same resting places each time and often returning to the exact same tree they started from. Thousands of people come to see this phenomenal sight. There is no other butterfly migration in the entire world like that of the monarch.

Are you interested in monarch migration? Log on to www.MonarchWatch.org. Here you will find Monarch Watch, which tells you all about monarchs and how you can help them survive.

HOW BUTTERFLIES CAME TO BE

Creator would often spend his days watching the people he had brought to life. But as the years passed, Creator noticed that no matter

Migration is the moving from one living site, country, or geographic region to another. Insects usually migrate to a better climate or better food supply and/or for reproductive purposes.

To *hibernate* is to "sleep" or remain still throughout a cold winter.

If you have "butterflies in your stomach," you are nervous, as if you had butterflies fluttering around within your body.

The ancient Aztecs of Mexico thought of the butterfly as a symbol of fire. The quivering of butterfly wings reminded them of flames.

Butterfly appearance and color are often tied to weather prediction in many cultures. In Great Britain, if the first butterfly of the season is white, that is a sign of good luck. If it is brown, that's bad luck. If it is yellow, that's a warning of sickness to come, but if it's gold-colored and flying near a sick person, that's a good sign. And if it's multicolored? A marriage will take place soon.

29

The beautiful monarch butterfly has one of the most amazing migrations in the animal kingdom.

how beautiful the children were, as they aged, they became wrinkled, weak, blind, and lame. Creator worried about this. He felt sorry for people and thought for a long time about what to do.

As Creator thought, he observed the peaceful blue sky dotted with white clouds. He admired the leaves, so many shades of green, gold, and brown. He found the flowers delightful, since they had more colors than the rainbow. And one day, as Creator watched the sun change from golden dawn to flaming sunset, he made a decision. "I want to create something beautiful that will not grow old," he said.

Creator took a bit of each of the beautiful colors from sky, clouds, leaves, flowers, and sunlight. He placed the colors in his magical bag. Then he gave the magical bag to the children to play with. When the children opened the bag, thousands of different butterflies flew out. They were blue, white, green, red, yellow, and purple, shining in the daylight as they took to the air.

The butterflies from the magic bag came out singing, which also made the children laugh. But soon jealous songbirds came to the Creator and complained. "We are the singers of this world," the songbirds reminded him. "It is not fair of you to give the butterflies both song and color."

So the Creator took song away from the butterflies, which is why, even though they are bright and beautiful and never change as they get older, they do not make a sound.

In Greek mythology, the beautiful Psyche, whose name also means "butterfly," was so lovely she attracted Cupid, the god of love.

In the ancient wisdom of most cultures, butterflies are to be treated with great kindness at all times.

In early North American folklore, if you wish on the first butterfly you see in spring, your wish will come true.

In some European folklore, the butterfly is a tiny fairy with multicolored wings. This fairy may steal butter and milk from the home.

Many of the Native American tribes use butterflies in their basket and beadwork design to represent the goodness of summer.

CRICKET

The most common North American cricket is the dark brown or black field cricket. Other commonly seen or heard crickets include the house cricket, California tree cricket, snowy tree cricket, and black-horned tree cricket.

There are also mole crickets and camel crickets. These crickets live primarily in dark places. Mole crickets have short antennae. They burrow underground and can fly well. Camel crickets have very long antennae, often longer than their bodies. They usually don't have wings. Camel crickets can be 1/2 inch to 2 inches (1 to 5 centimeters) long. Some camel crickets live in caves.

Some types of crickets live in ant nests. These crickets have learned the code that the ants use to ask for food. They tap antennae with worker ants in a certain pattern. If done correctly, the cricket gets fed. If done incorrectly, the cricket gets eaten.

The name "cricket" comes from the French word *criquer*, meaning "little creaker." Most crickets "sing" by scraping their wings together in a special way. The cricket rubs the hardened portion of its upper

Each type of cricket has its own special chirp. The house cricket, pictured here, chirps continuously.

forewing against the lower part of the forewing. This part has a thick vein with many tiny ridges, somewhat like a saw. The scraping noise that results is the cricket's "song."

Only male crickets make noise. Females are quiet. The song is used to court females, to establish a home territory, and to warn away predators such as birds. Each type of cricket has its own special song. The house cricket chirps continuously. The field cricket has a series of three chirps. The tree cricket goes "treet, treet, treet" or may have a continuous trill. Jerusalem camel crickets create a scratching noise. Mole crickets grunt.

A male mole cricket wants to make certain his mating call is heard. So, when digging a burrow, he makes it with a trumpet-shaped opening. This type of opening, like that on the musical instrument, enlarges sound. Tested just above a mole cricket's burrow, the mating call will register 90 decibels, as much noise as city traffic.

Depending on species, in the wild, adult crickets eat small insects such as aphids and caterpillars. Those living under rocks or below ground eat roots and dead insects. Young crickets, looking much like their parents, eat flowers, leaves, and young fruit.

SINGING CRICKETS OF CHINA

The earliest Chinese literature shows appreciation for singing insects such as katydids, cicadas, and crickets. It was said that when the cricket, called *Cu Zhi* ("encourage weaving") came indoors, it was surely October, and the women must hurry to finish their weaving so there would be warm cloth for the winter months.

People started keeping pet crickets in their homes during the Tang dynasty (A.D. 618 to 906) not only for the song, but also because a cricket in the house was supposed to bring good luck. Ladies in royal palaces kept their crickets in small golden cages, placing these near their beds in order to hear the songs at night. Professional cricket tenders were employed to keep the palace crickets healthy and ready to sing when the emperor had a special festival. The custom of keeping pet crickets is still quite common in many areas of China. People purchase the crickets, usually in bamboo or cardboard cages, at outdoor markets.

Within the home, cricket cages may be quite elaborate. While gourd cages are very popular, cages made of clay often have carvings of dragons, bats, the lotus flower, and the phoenix bird, all of which foretell some type of good luck.

In the Song dynasty (A.D. 960 to 1279), staged cricket fights began. This became a very popular sport, both with the emperor and upper classes and with the poorer people, too. People bet on the crickets, hoping their favorite would win. A cricket that won many fights was called a "Grand Master." There are many types of crickets, and not all were considered good for fighting, so some people became cricket breeders and specialists. After a while, people began to lose so much money from gambling that the government forbade cricket fighting. But it went on just the same and does so to this day. People write poems and stories about their favorite brave crickets.

A collection of cricket cages is in the Field Museum of Natural History in Chicago, and the Buffalo Museum of Science in New York.

THE DONKEY AND THE CRICKETS

A donkey was contentedly eating its dinner of leaves, bark, twigs, and grasses when it heard the sound of crickets chirping. This was such a

Temperature testing: If you count the number of cricket chirps in fifteen seconds, then add thirty-seven, this will tell you the approximate temperature in degrees Fahrenheit. Results vary a bit with the type of cricket.

The mole cricket has special forelegs for digging burrows.

delightful musical sound that the donkey decided to sing, too. Although it had been happy with its bray before, now the bray sounded loud and off-key.

"You sing so sweetly," the donkey told the crickets. "What do you eat that gives you such a silken voice?"

"We dine only on dew," the crickets replied.

That didn't sound too difficult to the donkey. "In no time at all, I will have a voice even better than that of the crickets," it thought.

So day after day, the donkey dined on nothing but dew and soon died of starvation.

DRAGONFLY

There are about 5,000 known dragonfly and damselfly species, with 450 species present in North America. The dragonfly's long wings may be clear with a netted appearance or banded with silver-white, brown, red, yellow, or bluish. Their bodies can be amber, reddish, blue, green, or brown and may have spots or markings of varying colors.

In North America, the green darner is one of the fastest and largest of the common dragonflies. It is about 3 inches (8 centimeters) long with a wingspan of 4 1/2 inches (11 centimeters). Other North American dragonflies include the brown-spotted yellow-wing, which flutters like a butterfly, the streak-winged red skimmer, the biddie, and the smallest North American dragonfly, the bluebell.

Dragonflies are found throughout the world in both tropical and cold climates. All have large heads, large bulging eyes, and stubby antennae. Each dragonfly has four large wings, two on each side. Dragonflies hold their wings horizontally on a slim body. Their close relative, the damselfly, holds its wings up when at rest. While dragonflies do not make any vocal sound, their wings make a whirring noise.

Nicknames for the dragonfly include "mosquito hawk" because it flies quickly and eats so many mosquitoes, "darning needle" and "darner" because of its shape, "club-tail," "horse stinger," and "snake doctor." Why "snake doctor"? An old story has dragonflies reviving dead snakes or warning snakes of approaching danger. As for "horse stinger," people thought that dragonflies around horses were going to sting the horses, but really the dragonflies were feeding on insects that pestered horses and cattle. The dragonfly does not sting or bite.

The large green darner is one of the most noticeable dragonflies.

Native Americans thought dragonflies were the souls of the dead returning to earth. In Japanese Buddhist tradition, it's specifically red dragonflies that symbolize the return of the dead to their former homes. The presence of dragonflies foretells happiness, and the dragonfly is also a symbol of victory in battle. In many cultures, it is considered bad luck to kill a dragonfly.

Many dragonfly species today are endangered due to the loss of their wetland habitat. In 1985, the first dragonfly sanctuary was established in Japan. An important part of the sanctuary are the ponds where dragonflies can live safely. *Tombo* is the Japanese word for dragonfly.

Dragonflies usually live or fly near slow rivers, ponds, and lakes, although they may travel for many miles in order to feed. Dragonflies are quite beneficial to the environment. They eat mosquitoes, flies, gnats, and other flying insects. In just thirty minutes, a dragonfly can eat its own weight in insects. Dragonflies can fly both forward and backward. All dragonflies fly quickly. Flight speed is combined with spiny legs that dangle down forming a basketlike shape, allowing them to rapidly scoop up flying insect meals. Once an insect has been trapped, the legs bring the insect to the mouth and powerful jaws tear the *prey* apart. Many scientists think that dragonflies have the best vision of any insect.

The largest dragonfly that ever lived flew in the Permian period, 230 million years ago, even before the Age of Dinosaurs. It had a wingspan of about 30 inches (76 centimeters). Fossils show that it looked quite like our modern dragonfly, except for size. Today, the world's largest dragonfly species lives in South America. It has a 7 1/2-inch (19-centimeter) wingspan. The largest North American dragonflies have a nearly 6-inch (15-centimeter) wingspan. Body length on the larger dragonflies can reach 6 inches (15 centimeters).

What's the smallest dragonfly? A Malaysian dragonfly is just 3/5 inch (15 millimeters) long.

How fast can a dragonfly fly? There's all sorts of discussion about that. A lot depends on how long the dragonfly can keep up the speed, plus wind and other weather factors. A large dragonfly can fly 24 miles (39 kilometers) per hour. However, you may see printed records that claim dragonflies have been clocked in flight, for short distances, at up to 60 miles (97 kilometers) per hour.

If you see two dragonflies holding onto each other while flying, they are probably mating. Female dragonflies place their eggs in or near water, often on floating plants. Their young, called naiads, or

The smaller, more slender damselfly is related to the dragonfly, and sometimes confused with it.

nymphs, do not look at all like the adults. Dragonfly nymphs may molt from ten to fifteen times before becoming adults. The young live in muddy river bottoms under plants and breathe through gills. They eat water insects of all kinds as well as small fish and tadpoles. One dragonfly nymph was recorded as eating 3,037 mosquito larvae in a year!

In a few months to a few years, depending on species, the naiads climb out of the water and molt a final time. To avoid predators such as frogs and birds, they often come out after dark. When the last molt is complete, the nymphs finally look like adults.

HOW THE DRAGONFLY CAME TO BE

Long ago, a boy loved a pretty girl. But she only liked handsome warriors. The boy was plain and not very strong. He became very sad. One night the boy climbed a high mountain and lay down on a large rock. "Why am I so ugly?" he wondered. He prayed and sang, asking the Great Spirit to make him beautiful in the eyes of his beloved. Finally he fell asleep.

The Great Spirit heard the prayers. Using moonlight and cobwebs, he created four long wings. Then he touched the sleeping boy and made his body lighter than air.

The next morning, the boy awoke. He felt different, lighter. When he arose and stretched, he suddenly began flying. His flight was swift and strong. The boy flew to the stream and looked at himself. He was satisfied. Then he flew to his beloved.

"How beautiful," she exclaimed. And ever afterward, she was interested only in warriors who were as swift and beautiful as the dragonfly—which none were.

FIREFLY

Fireflies aren't flies, nor are they bugs, as their other common name, lightning bug, suggests. They are 1/4- to 3/4-inch (6- to 19-millimeter) winged beetles which often have a light-producing organ, sometimes called a "taillight" or "lantern," located on the tail section of their abdomen. The light given off may be whitish, yellow, green, or reddish. It depends on which type of firefly beetle is flashing.

There are about two thousand different firefly members of the *Lampyridae* family. *Lampyridae* is a very old Latin word meaning "shining fire." This same Latin word also gave rise to the word "lamp."

What makes a firefly light up? The light-producing organ has many air tubes. It also has cells containing a substance called luciferin. When oxygen enters the air tubes, it comes in contact with the luciferin. A chemical reaction takes place, helped along by an *enzyme* called luciferace. The chemical reaction causes energy to be given off in the form of light. What causes the flashing pattern? Each firefly species can control the amount of oxygen going to its light organ.

Fireflies are most commonly seen from spring until early autumn.

An *enzyme* is a protein substance produced by living cells that is necessary to body functioning. There are many different types of enzymes.

In the southern part of the United States, a firefly entering a home means that good luck is on the way or that a stranger will arrive soon.

43

In Japan, poets have written about firefly beauty for more than a thousand years. There are still festivals held to honor the firefly, often held in August when the most fireflies are about. Up to 10,000 people may attend a firefly festival.

Do the words "luciferin" and "luciferace" seem familiar? They were taken from the name Lucifer. In mythology, Lucifer is the bearer of light.

An ancient tradition warns that anyone who kills a glow-worm risks ending a love affair and possibly even causing a lover's death.

If a farmer wants a consistently good crop, a glowworm should be kept in the house.

People have been curious about firefly light for a very long time. Before modern scientists discovered the special cells in a firefly's light-producing organ, people in Europe sometimes thought the little lights were turned off and on when the fireflies opened and closed their wings.

This view of the underside of a firefly clearly shows the whitish light-producing organ in its abdomen.

When the sun starts to set, females, who usually do not fly, crawl up from where they live on the ground to near the top of a blade of grass or similar greenery. The males come courting. They fly slowly, usually just a few inches to a few feet off the ground. Blink, blink, go their lights.

Each of the firefly species has its own communication pattern, or blinking code. It may vary by light color or brightness, by the number of flashes in a row, by the length of time between flashes, and by how long each flash lasts. In addition, the males may fly at various heights and in varying flight patterns.

The purpose of this variation is so a female can identify a male of her own species. When she does, she flashes back the same signal. The males and females repeat this signal several times. When the time is right, the male flies over to the female and touches her with his antennae to double-check she has the correct species scent. Then mating takes place.

Not all fireflies have this mating procedure. A few species are great mimics. Instead of returning only the signal of a male in the same species, the females mimics the signal of just about any male firefly. When the wrong male lands next to her, hoping to mate, he gets pounced on and becomes a meal.

After mating, the female places from one hundred to five hundred eggs on damp soil. Small larvae emerge in about a month. The larvae live in damp places under tree bark or decaying vegetation on the ground. They feed on smaller insect larvae, earthworms, slugs, and snails. After a year or two, the larvae slowly change into pupae. Once they do, adult fireflies emerge just two weeks later. Adult firefly beetles may or may not eat, depending on the species. They live only about a week.

Firefly eggs may be luminous, or give off a steady light. Firefly larvae,

In Italy, children used to catch a firefly and keep it under a glass overnight, hoping in the morning that they would find a coin instead of a firefly. Children of long ago, and now, often collect fireflies in a jar to watch them blink. The jar should have holes in the top so the fireflies get oxygen. And, of course, the fireflies should be set free after a short while.

A firefly larva, sometimes called a glowworm, gives off a steady, pale light.

sometimes called glowworms, may also give off a steady pale light. Scientists are not quite sure why this happens.

Where can you find fireflies? Mostly in meadows and open woodland. You may even see a firefly but not know it. Not all fireflies give off light.

There are also other insects that give off light. There are fire beetles that are sometimes called fireflies, but belong to a different family known as click beetles. They give off a much brighter, steady light than true fireflies.

There's also a gnat that has luminous larvae with a bluish light. These larvae are sometimes also called glowworms, fireflies, or lightning bugs.

True fireflies have a blinking light. Other luminous insects give off a steady light.

WHY FIREFLY CARRIES A LIGHT

Alitaptap the Firefly and Lamok the Mosquito did not get along at all. Lamok kept chasing Alitaptap. Lamok had a dagger (stinger) and Alitaptap was afraid of him. So Alitaptap took to carrying around a torch (taillight) so he could watch out for the dangerous Lamok. The animals around them got angry at Alitaptap for carrying fire, saying that was dangerous. Alitaptap explained that he needed the light to protect himself against Lamok's dagger. The other animals didn't like Lamok's dagger either, so they put him in jail. While Lamok was in jail, he lost his voice. Today the male mosquito is silent and the firefly still carries a light.

FLEA

There are more than two thousand flea species in the world. Each flea has a hollow, needlelike, sucking mouthpart. When the flea lands on a host animal, including a human, its mouthpart makes a tiny hole in the animal's skin. The flea then sucks up blood. Some people are more sensitive to flea bites than others. On their skin, bite areas may become itchy red dots.

There are fleas that prefer feasting on goats, skunks, lizards, swallows, ducks, rabbits, dogs, cats, rats, pigeons, spiny anteaters, and hedgehogs. However most, but not all, fleas will bite almost any warm-blooded animal if they are hungry. But a flea expert can look at a flea under a microscope and tell what its normal host is. Each flea species looks slightly different.

Many fleas can live more than two years if well fed. The oldest flea on record is a Russian bird flea. It lived for four years and twenty-seven days. One of the largest fleas on record was found in a mountain beaver's nest. This female flea measured 3/10 inch (8 millimeters).

Some scientists like to measure how far a flea can jump. Most fleas only jump about 1 1/2 inches (4 centimeters). But there are super

This flea belongs to the species that feeds on the blood of cats.

jumpers, such as one of the human fleas. A very lively human flea can jump from 7 to 12 inches (18 to 30 centimeters) into the air and make a long jump of 13 inches (33 centimeters). A human being would have to jump 450 feet (137 meters) into the air and long jump 700 feet (213 meters) to match the athletic ability of a flea.

Not all fleas hop. Those living on tree animals might fall while hopping. So squirrel, bat, and bird fleas tend to crawl.

After mating, female fleas lay their whitish eggs on the host animal. The eggs drop off as the animal moves about. The female flea may also lay her eggs in the nest or bed of the host animal. The wormlike larvae are a dull white color. They feed on decaying animal or vegetable matter. Flea larvae spin sticky silken cocoons that are soon covered with dirt and dust.

Depending on the type of flea, the weather, and feeding prospects, adult fleas may emerge in a few days or take a lot longer. People are often surprised, when entering a house that has been completely empty for some time, to find a batch of newly hatched hungry fleas awaiting their first meal.

PAN-GU

Pan-gu, a dwarf, was the first living thing in the entire universe. He came into being within an egg. Pan-gu grew 10 feet (3 meters) per day. As he grew, he pushed the top part of the egg upward, where it formed the sky. The bottom part of the egg formed the Earth. Pan-gu grew for 13,000 years, then burst apart. His eyes became the sun and moon. His blood turned into seas and rivers. His voice became thunder and his breath became the wind. His sweat changed into rain and dew. His hair turned into trees and grasses. And the fleas that had been living on Pan-gu's skin became the ancestors of the human race.

FLY

There are about 86,000 species of flies with about 16,300 species living in North America. They include the common houseflies, crane flies, midges, mosquitoes, fungus gnats, horseflies, robber flies, dance flies, long-legged flies, thick-headed flies, fruit flies, marsh flies, seaweed flies, vinegar flies, louse flies, and fringe-legged Tachinid flies, among many others.

How do you know an insect is a fly? Flies have only one pair of normal-appearing wings. The second pair, just behind the first, looks like little bumps. These are used as stabilizers, or balancers, during flight.

Horse flies can be an inch (2.5 centimeters) long, and can have brightly colored eyes. Their flight is often silent. Male horse flies feed on flower pollen and nectar. Females bite animals to obtain a blood meal. The protein in blood is necessary for female egg-laying success.

Robber flies can be more than an inch (2.5 centimeters) long. They are often long and skinny, with large bulging eyes, and covered in bristles. Robber flies feed on insects. One reason given for the

Flies are usually a sign of something bad. The more flies there are in your neighborhood, the worse things will be. If flies are in your home, you should open a window or door and ask the good spirits of the Earth to remove all the bad spirits and bad bugs. Should flies remain, or to prevent their appearance in the first place, superstition is that you should hang three eggs over the front door on Ash Wednesday.

51

The larger robber fly makes a quick meal out of a housefly.

"robber" name is that these flies often wait until a prey insect is resting, then pounce on it from above, feeding on its body fluids. Or they may pounce on their prey in flight, hold on to the insect, rest on a twig, and suck it dry in seconds.

Bee flies, stout and about 1/2 inch (1 centimeter) long, look somewhat like bees but act more like hummingbirds, flitting around flowers and hovering in midair. These furry-looking flies can be quite pretty, with patterned wings and silvery bristles. Adults feed on flower nectar and are helpful pollinators. Bee fly larvae feed on the eggs of other insects, including grasshopper and wasp eggs. You may see bee flies enjoying the sunshine by resting, with wings outstretched, on a flower.

Hover flies, often called flower flies, are between 1/4 and 3/4 inch (6 and 19 millimeters) long. They are often mistaken for bees or wasps since many are yellow and black, and they hover around flowers with a quiet buzzing sound. They suck up flower nectar and are important pollinators. Hover fly larvae often feed on pest insects such as aphids and are important in controlling pest insect populations.

Pomace flies, often called fruit flies, are the tiny flies 1/16 to 1/8 inch (1.6 to 3 millimeters) long, that seem to appear like magic around decaying fruits and vegetables. Adults drink nectar and other sugary matter, and the young feed on the yeasts that are part of decaying fruit juices. In the wild they are useful scavengers, breaking down rotting plant material.

A few species of fruit flies, such as the vinegar fly, are often raised in schools and laboratories. They have proved useful in genetic research because they are easily reared and multiply very rapidly. Each female produces one hundred or more eggs. These hatch in two days and become reproducing adults within two weeks. And if all the offspring survived? Within a year, if the fruit flies were packed together, they

There is a common saying about a successful eavesdropper being like a fly on the wall. In an ancient Sumerian legend, Inanna, queen of heaven, sent a fly as her messenger to rescue her husband, Dumuzi, from the underworld. When the fly was successful, she asked it what it wanted as a reward. The fly wanted to become well educated. Inanna rewarded the fly by allowing it to enter any tavern, where it could hear the conversations of the wise and well educated without being noticed.

In Europe and South America, many people once believed that flies were the souls of the dead.

Everyone can recognize the all-too-familiar housefly.

would form a ball 96 million miles wide.

Another type of fruit fly has a colorfully patterned body and patterned wings. These are sometimes called peacock flies, and a few species can be severe agricultural pests. You may have heard of these fruit flies under names such as medfly (Mediterranean fruit fly), walnut husk fly, and apple maggot fly.

Shore flies are the blackish flies found at the seashore and at the edges of ponds and lakes. You may see seaweed flies at the beach, too. Seaweed flies tend to stay on decaying seaweed and are very important food for shorebirds.

HOUSEFLIES

At least 98 percent of flies caught in the house are houseflies. Houseflies can transmit sixty-five diseases, including cholera, dysentery, anthrax, and typhoid fever. As many as six million bacteria can be carried on a housefly's body and some can be left behind where it travels. Houseflies may vomit part of recently eaten food, possibly from contaminated garbage areas, onto the food and people they come in contact with. They can also transmit parasitic worms to people, including pinworms, some tapeworms, and hookworms.

The common housefly has a very short life span. Males live only about two weeks, and females four weeks. However, houseflies multiply very rapidly. Scientists have tried to figure out how many flies would result from an original pair if none died. In just one summer, there might be more than 6 trillion houseflies from just that one pair and its descendants.

How does a housefly walk up walls so easily? On each of the fly's

During World War II, intensive, and expensive, research was done on the various Syrphid flies to see how they balanced themselves during flight. It was hoped the results could be applied to airplanes. But insect flight, as it was later discovered, is quite different from that of airplanes because insects are so much smaller.

If a housefly falls into your drink, that's supposed to be lucky. So are flies found in your house around Christmas. It is unusual for flies to survive cold weather. Those that do are lucky—therefore, they should not be swatted.

six feet there are small pads. On each of these pads there are hundreds of tiny hollow hairs. The fly produces a gluelike substance that comes down through these hairs onto the foot pads. It helps the fly stick to the wall or windowpane.

THE CAMEL AND THE FLY

There once was a fly with a very high opinion of itself. One day, while scouting for food, it saw a camel carrying a large load. "I will rest there," thought the fly. It sat on the camel's back, and thought even more highly of itself, because now it was even taller than the great camel. After a very long journey, the camel rested. The fly flew to the ground. "Thank you for the ride," it said. "I hope I have not been too heavy a burden."

"I did not know you were there, and so I won't feel any different now that you are gone," said the camel.

Moral: He who is nothing but thinks he is something is still nothing.

GRASSHOPPER

There are about 9,800 grasshopper species worldwide. The common names for grasshoppers can become confusing. The Latin word for grasshopper is *locust*. Some people call them grasshoppers, others locusts. Both names are correct. Usually, however, it's the grasshoppers with antennae shorter than their bodies, the short-horned grasshoppers, that are known as locusts. These include the panther-spotted grasshopper, horse lubber, painted grasshopper, and the Alutacea bird grasshopper.

In late fall, adult males create a tune to attract a female of the same species. Grasshoppers do not have a voice, but "singing" is what their "chirring" sound is often called. Males rub their hind legs against their wings, or their hind wings against their front wings, to create sound. Each species has its own special tune.

After mating, the female places groups of eggs, or pods, in soil. Each pod contains from twenty to 120 eggs. Both she and the male usually die by the time cold weather arrives. When the weather warms up in spring, the young emerge. They usually look somewhat like their parents.

In China, grasshoppers are symbols of good luck and happiness. If you see a grasshopper, according to some, it means it is time for you to take chances and "leap forward."

In China, there were locust gods. These gods hopefully would imprison destructive locusts in gourds.

A Hopi myth concerns Locust, the supernatural patron of the Hopi flute society. Since Locust cannot be struck by lightning, medicine made from locusts is good for healing wounds.

The colorful painted grasshopper is one of the species commonly known as a locust.

At first the young don't have wings. Later, after several molts, their wings grow. Some grasshopper species fly. Others just jump. Each jump can be a very long one, sometimes twenty times the grasshopper's body length. A grasshopper's hind legs are exceptionally strong.

Adult grasshoppers range in size from 1/2 inch to 6 inches (1 to 15 centimeters). While the coloring of many grasshoppers matches their surroundings (green in fields, beige on deserts and beaches) some have yellow, red, green, white, pink, black, or blue markings.

In most places throughout the world, grasshoppers are considered pests. Their mouthparts can chew almost every type of plant material. When there are millions of grasshoppers feeding in an area, no plant life of any kind can remain.

When there is not enough food in one area, some grasshopper species fly to new feeding sites. Locusts who travel are often called migratory locusts. One of the longest recorded insect migrations, 2,000 miles (3,200 kilometers), was accomplished by desert locusts. The desert locust is considered by many to be the most destructive insect in the world. These locusts live in dry areas of Pakistan, India, the Middle East, and Africa. They often migrate in enormous groups that darken the sky for several days. One swarm was estimated to include 250 billion desert locusts. Since a locust can eat its own weight in food each day, a swarm can eat 6,000 pounds (2,700 kilograms) of food per day, which can devastate farmers' crops.

GRASSHOPPER AND THE ANTS

Grasshopper was a lazy fellow. He sang all summer's day. He ate whatever leaves and grain were nearby. Sometimes he just jumped from place to place for the fun of it.

In West Africa, there was a ceremony to rid an area of locusts. A special person was dressed in fine clothing and decorations, then sent away with strict instructions not to return. It was hoped that the locusts would follow that person and never return.

In the 1870s, Rocky Mountain locusts arrived in the farmland of some midwestern states. They ate every leaf, grass blade, and twig, so cattle and horses could not find food. A bounty was placed on them, one dollar for a bushel or large box of young locusts, five dollars for a bushel of egg pods.

Over the centuries, enormous effort has gone into ridding an area of locusts. Long ago in Europe, people tried to frighten locust swarms away by ringing church bells, firing guns, burning stinking sulfur, and blowing trumpets, but it didn't help.

In India, a custom was to capture one locust and put a drop of red lead on its forehead before letting it go. It was hoped that the rest of the horde would depart with this special locust.

59

The powerful hind legs of a grasshopper are its most amazing feature. This is a slant-faced grasshopper.

Summer became autumn. When Grasshopper had nothing better to do, he would sit on a branch and watch the busy ants. To and fro they went, hurry, hurry, carrying food in their mouths for their young. "We save some food, too," said the ants.

"There is plenty of food," said Grasshopper. "Why save it?"

"In winter, food is hard to find," said the ants.

"Winter is a long time away," said Grasshopper. "I'd rather have a good time now, while I have the chance. Why don't you join me?"

But the ants kept going to and fro, hurry, hurry.

Grasshopper hopped away. "Ants work too hard," he said. "Not me. I'm smart."

Soon snow covered the ground. There were no leaves. There was no grain. Grasshopper became quite hungry. One very cold day, Grasshopper hopped slowly to the ant nest. "May I have something to eat?" he begged.

"No," said the ants. "You were loafing last summer when we were working."

"I wasn't loafing," argued Grasshopper. "I was singing and playing."

"Then sing and play all winter," the ants replied.

Grasshopper sat on a snow-covered branch. He got thinner and thinner. Finally the ants took pity on him and gave him something to eat.

"Thank you," said Grasshopper. "You have saved my life."

"We have kept you alive as a lesson for our children," the ants replied. "Grasshoppers may be necessary to have around. They are a reminder of what happens when one does not prepare for hard times."

Locust infestations have long been associated with plague outbreaks. While locusts don't carry disease, they can cause extreme food shortages. Lack of food can weaken a population, and disease may take hold where it wouldn't otherwise do so.

For many thousands of years, in many parts of the world, some grasshopper species have been used as food. Grasshoppers may be fried in butter and seasoned with pepper and salt, cooked with curry for extra flavor, ground into cereal form from which cakes are made, dried as a protein snack for winter, or boiled and spread on house roofs to dry.

Old farm lore says that grasshoppers can predict the weather. If many grasshoppers appear in one area, the weather will be hot and dry, and farmers should prepare for a drought. Although this is part of folklore, it has a scientific base. If the weather has been damp, many grasshopper eggs may be destroyed by disease. In dry weather, more eggs survive to produce young. So larger numbers of grasshoppers appear during drought periods.

MOSQUITO

What attracts a mosquito looking for a blood meal? Perfume, including scented soaps, perspiration, body heat, and carbon dioxide in exhaled breath. In total darkness, a mosquito can sense the breath of a large animal up to 40 yards (37 meters) away. Why do mosquitoes bite some people and not others? Each person has a different body chemistry, and mosquitoes can be quite picky. Not only are they choosy about which animal or person to bite, some species even have favorite biting spots, such as the forehead.

Not all mosquitoes feed on animal blood. There are about 2,700 mosquito species worldwide. Males feed on *honeydew* and flower nectar. Most females prefer a blood meal. The female mosquito usually needs the protein in blood to lay eggs. She will lay eggs in almost any type of standing water, warm or cold. Usually the eggs hatch within a few days or weeks. Mosquitoes in dry climates deposit eggs with thicker shells. These eggs won't hatch until rains come, which may take a year or even up to ten years.

This mosquito looks scary magnified many times over, and it should: It belongs to the species that transmits yellow fever.

One scientist tried to figure out how many mosquitoes would be produced from one female with a month-long life span. If this female lays about ten egg batches with two hundred eggs in each batch, and each of the young begins producing its own egg batches at two weeks, in five generations, if all the mosquitoes survived, there would be 20 million mosquitoes that originated from just the one original female.

A mosquito's wings can beat up to six hundred times per second, depending on the species. A mosquito can fly sideways, backward, and upside down. For mating purposes, female mosquitoes attract male mosquitoes by a species-specific wingbeat buzz.

The feeding habits of mosquitoes vary. One species of tropical mosquito rests on a tree trunk waiting for ants to crawl by. The mosquito flies over to an ant and holds on to it with its two front legs. The mosquito strokes the ant with its antennae, encouraging the ant to throw up the contents of its stomach so the mosquito can get a free meal. The ant is not allowed to move until it gives the mosquito a bit of food.

Many animals feed on mosquitoes, including dragonflies, salamanders, swallows, ducks, bats, and toads. People also destroy mosquitoes. In addition to swatting at them, many people get rid of mosquito breeding sites such as water-containing flowerpots, leaf-filled house gutters, old tires, food cans, ditches, puddles, and any other container that holds standing water. Just one puddle of standing water can hold more than five hundred "wigglers," or tiny, wiggly, wormlike mosquito larvae.

There are about sixty mosquito species that transmit disease of some type. In some countries, it is difficult to get rid of mosquito

One spring, Canadian researchers working in the Arctic wanted to find out how many mosquito bites they would get in one minute if they sat still. In the Arctic spring, the melting snow encourages all local mosquitoes to hatch at the same time. The count was about nine thousand bites per person in one minute.

A modern scientist wanted to see what aromas attracted mosquitoes. Smelly socks and Limburger cheese were on top of the list.

In Romania, people say that if you want angels in your house, you must drive away any mosquitoes, as angels cannot enter when mosquitoes are present.

A mosquito has a short life span but can produce many, many young in that time. In this picture, two mosquitoes are mating.

breeding sites. In these countries, diseases such as malaria, yellow fever, elephantiasis, heartworm, filariasis, dengue fever, and encephalitis, among other diseases, still exist. Mosquito-transmitted encephalitis still exists in the United States. Certain mosquito species carry the disease organisms within their saliva, transferring it when they bite. While most mosquitoes bite at night, the yellow-fever mosquito and a few others will bite during the day.

HOW MOSQUITOES CAME TO BE

A long time ago, there was a man-eating giant who killed the parents of a boy. The monster then tried to kill the boy, but he ran away as fast as he could.

The boy ran a great distance. Kind relatives took care of him until he grew up. One day he heard that the monster was still frightening people where he used to live. The young man was now strong and brave. He searched for the giant and killed it. But the giant came to life again. The young man killed the giant again and again. But each time the giant was able to return.

The next time the young man killed the giant, he burned the body, thinking this would end the giant's horrible deeds once and for all. But from the place where the giant had been destroyed, a voice cried out that even if its body was gone, it would find a way to torment people.

As the voice spoke, the wind came and scattered the giant's ashes into the air. The ashes became mosquitoes, which feed on the blood of people and animals, tormenting people all over the world.

Mosquitoes have, at times, changed the course of history. The French general Napoleon, having seen the death rate from mosquito-transmitted malaria, decided he could not successfully maintain a large army in any warm climate. So how was he to protect the hot and humid Louisiana Territory, which he acquired in his battles with Spain? In 1803, Napoleon decided to sell Louisiana to the United States. The price: about 4 cents an acre (0.4 hectare), a real bargain even then. Napoleon thought he was getting the best of the deal, but the Americans later got rid of most of the disease-carrying mosquitoes.

Early American Pilgrims wrote about "muskets" (their name for mosquitoes) and how terribly annoying they were.

The common malaria-carrying mosquito can fly 25 miles (40 kilometers) during its spring flights.

66

WASP

There are thousands of different types of wasps, but the one most people are familiar with is the yellow jacket. Measuring about 1/2 to 1 inch (1 to 3 centimeters) long, these wasps are striped yellow and black. In the insect world, this is a caution signal that says "stay away." Each yellow jacket has a stinger at its back end. Unlike the honeybee, which usually will not sting unless it is annoyed, stings just once, and then dies, the female yellow jacket can sting multiple times without much reason. Her stinger does not have barbs, so it is easily withdrawn by the wasp for future use.

Yellow jackets usually nest at ground level, sometimes in holes in the ground left by gophers or field mice. They may also be found in the hollows of tree stumps and fallen logs or in rock walls. Occasionally nests are made in bushes and trees. When people get stung by wasps, it is often because they have accidentally stepped on a wasp nest while walking through a meadow or on a forest path.

In the spring, fertilized female wasps (queens), begin chewing on wood and leaf fragments, mixing them with saliva to form a thin,

Yellow jackets swarm around their nest.

paperlike material from which they construct their nests. The early nests are only about an inch (3 centimeters) wide and composed of a few hexagonal (six-sided) cells glued together with saliva. The first eggs are placed in the cells. When the young, or grubs, emerge, the queen feeds them. She catches insects, partially chews them, then brings them back to the nest. The grubs pupate, developing into workers a few weeks later. These help to enlarge the nest. A nest may become 12 inches (30 centimeters) wide or even wider. A nest found in New Zealand measured 15 feet (5 meters) high and 5 feet (2 meters) wide.

In the fall, things slow down. Female wasps mate with the males (drones), and the wasps in the nest die or scatter. In many areas, yellow jackets become a nuisance around houses and picnic grounds. Yellow jacket adults usually dine on flower nectar. But now the flowers are gone, and the wasps are hungry.

By winter, all are dead except for a few queens who have hidden in cracks around trees, usually in wooded areas. Here the queens will rest until the following spring.

Sometimes the hornet, another type of wasp, is confused with the yellow jacket. The hornet creates its large, round, pear-shaped paper nests above ground, under the eaves of houses or hanging from a large tree limb. The nests can be seen when the tree's leaves fall. While nests are usually vacant by the time cold weather arrives, it's best not to get too close to them. Hornets do not usually attack unless their nest is threatened, but they are extremely protective of their nest and will sting multiple times. The sting is quite painful.

Wasps and hornets eat nectar and fruit juices. They are beneficial pollinators and kill many harmful insects.

A spider wasp attacks its prey, a wolf spider.

Other wasps you may see include the blue-black spider wasp, steel-blue cricket hunter, great golden digger wasp, cicada killer, sand wasp, red velvet-ant, and the potter wasp.

Wasps' nests vary quite a bit. A potter wasp's nest looks like a small clay jar. Paper wasps make nests that look like upside-down tables. Gall wasps lay eggs in plants that form a swelling, or gall, around the eggs. Cuckoo wasps place their eggs in the nests of bees or other wasps.

The world's largest wasps live in South America. They are the spider-hunting wasps, and they can reach 2 1/2 inches (6 centimeters) long with a wingspan of 4 inches (10 centimeters).

There are also tiny parasitic wasps. Parasitic wasps may place their eggs in the eggs of other tiny insects, or in the insect itself. When the wasp young emerge, they feed on the egg or body parts of their host insect. Parasitic wasps, although seldom seen because of their size, are beneficial because they destroy pests harmful to crops.

THE WASP AS JUDGE

Female honeybee workers were in a big argument with the male honeybee drones of their hive. The workers had, over the spring and summer, collected lots of nectar and made it into honey. Now the lazy drones, who hadn't done anything, were claiming that all this honey was theirs.

Finally they all went to court, where Wasp was the judge. Wasp knew a lot about bees, but to do his job well, he studied them even more, including their body shape and color. To Wasp, the workers and the drones looked alike. So he couldn't understand why they were fussing.

However, since his job was to make a decision, he gave each side a task. "Here are some wax cells for storing honey," Wasp said, handing them to the workers and to the drones. "Each of you will collect nectar and make it into honey to fill these honeycombs. I will then test the honey and see which is the same as that in your hive. That way I will know who is the owner of the honey you are arguing about."

The worker bees immediately agreed, but the drones immediately refused.

"Well, then," said Wasp, "it is quite clear who collected and made the honey." And with that, Wasp decided that the honey belonged to the worker bees.

SOURCES

ANT: "The Ant Men" was retold and adapted from information provided on the Greek Mythology Link [www.has.brown.edu/~maicar/Aeacus.html]; The Bestiary [ww2.netnitco.net/users/legend01/ant.html]; Classical Mythology [wysiwyg://30/http://longman.awl.com/mythology/glossaries/character_a.asp]; *Dictionary of Mythology,* ed. Bergen Evans (NY: Dell Publishing, 1970); *The Wordsworth Dictionary of Phrase & Fable* (London: Wordsworth, 1970); and Anthony S. Mercatante, *Zoo of the Gods* (New York: Harper & Row, 1999).

BEE: The Filipino vignette was summarized from information provided in *Philippine Folk Literature: The Myths,* ed. Damiana L. Eugenio (Quezon City: University of the Philippines Press, 1993). The book's editor credits the story to "A Study of Representative Tales of Illocos Norte" (Master's thesis, FEU, 1958).

The Australian vignette was summarized from information in *Australian Legendary Tales,* ed. Mrs. K. Langloh Parker (London: Bodley Head, 1978).

The fourth-century Greek vignette was summarized from information provided in *Babrius and Phaedrus,* ed. and trans. Ben Edwin Perry (London: Harvard University Press, 1965); and P.E. Widdows, *The Fables of Phaedrus* (Austin: University of Texas Press, 1992).

BEETLE: "Water Beetle Creates the World" was adapted and retold from information provided in *Cultural Entomology Digest*—Beetles as Religious Symbols [www.insects.org/ced2beetles_rel_sym.html]; and *Myths and Legends of the Great Plains,* ed. Katharine Berry Judson (Chicago: A.C. McClurg, 1913).

The Native American star tale was adapted from *Funk & Wagnalls Standard Dictionary of Folklore, Mythology and Legend,* ed. Maria Leach (New York: Funk & Wagnalls, 1972), referenced to the Sia Indians of North America.

BUTTERFLY: "How Butterflies Came to Be" was adapted and retold from information provided in *Cultural Entomology Digest* (4-Lepidoptera) in the Mythology of Native Americans [www.insects.org/ced4/mythology.html];

Long Ago Told Legends of the Papago Indians, arr. Harold Bell Wright, with legends attributed to the collection of Mrs. Katherine Kit (New York: Appleton, 1929); William Ramsay Smith, *Aborigine Myths and Legends,* (London: Random House, 1996); and *American Indian Myths and Legends,* eds. Richard Erdoes and Alfonso Ortiz (New York: Pantheon Books, 1984).

CRICKET: This story, originally titled "The Ass and the Cricket," was adapted and retold from information provided in *Babrius and Phaedrus*; *The Fables of Phaedrus*; *The Complete Fables of Jean de la Fontaine*, ed. Norman Spector (Evanston, IL: Northwestern University Press, 1988); and *Aesop's Fables* ["The Ass and the Grasshoppers"], trans. Thomas James and George Tyler Townsend (Franklin Center, PA: The Franklin Library, 1982).

DRAGONFLY: "How the Dragonfly Came to Be" was adapted and retold from information provided in *Long Ago Told Legends of the Papago Indians*.

FIREFLY: "Why Firefly Carries a Light" was adapted and retold from information provided in *Folk Culture of the Central Visayas* (Quezon City: Ministry of Education, Republic of the Philippines, 1986); *Once in the First Times: Folk Tales from the Philippines*, retold by Elizabeth Hough Sechrist (Philadelphia: Macrae Smith, 1969); and *Funk & Wagnalls Standard Dictionary of Folklore, Mythology and Legend*.

FLEA: "Pan-Gu" was adapted and retold from information provided in *Encyclopedia Mythica*, s.v. "Pan-Gu" [www.pantheon.org/mythica/articles/p/pan-gu.html]; *Encyclopedia Mythica*, s.v. "creation myths" [www.pantheon.org/mythica/articles/c/creation_myths.html]; and *Who is P'an Ku?* [fs.broward.cc.fl.us/south/english/pankuhistory.html].

FLY: "The Camel and the Fly" was adapted and retold from information provided in *100 World's Greatest Fables*, trans. Chen Der and Lee Chung (Sun Publishing,1987); and *Aesop's Fables* ["The Gnat and the Bull"].

GRASSHOPPER: "Grasshopper and the Ants" was adapted and retold from information provided in A.W. Reed, *Maori Fables and Legendary Tales* (Sydney, Australia: 1992); Bobby Lake-Thom, *Spirits of the Earth* (New York: Penguin, 1991); *Zoo of the Gods; Funk & Wagnalls Standard Dictionary of Folklore, Mythology and Legend*; and Stith Thompson, *Motif*

Index of Folk Literature (London: Indiana University Press, 1975. [This source mentions at least three North American Indian borrowings of this Asiatic-European story].

MOSQUITO: "How Mosquitoes Came to Be" was adapted and retold from information provided in *Mythology of All Races*, ed. Canon John Arnott MacCulloch (New York: Cooper Square Publishers, 1964) [Siberian mythology]; and *Funk & Wagnalls Standard Dictionary of Folklore, Mythology and Legend*, referenced to North Pacific Coast and Plains Indians.

WASP: Variations of "The Wasp as Judge" were found in *The Complete Fables of Jean de la Fontaine*, told as "The Hornets and the Honeybees"; Angelo de Gubernatis, *Zoological Mythology* (1872; reprint, New York: Arno Press, 1978); *Funk & Wagnalls Standard Dictionary of Folklore, Mythology and Legend*, referenced to Phaedrus of Macedonia, first century A.D.

FURTHER READING

Aesop's Fables, trans. Thomas James and George Tyler Townsend. Franklin Center, PA: The Franklin Library, 1982.

Agosta, William. *Bombardier Beetles and Fever Trees.* New York: Addison-Wesley, 1996.

Berenbaum, May R. *Ninety-Nine Gnats, Nits and Nibblers.* Chicago: University of Illinois Press, 1989.

Evans, Bergen, ed. *Dictionary of Mythology.* New York: Dell, 1970.

Evans, Howard Ensign. *Life on a Little Known Planet.* New York: Dell, 1968.

Mercatante, Anthony S. *Zoo of the Gods.* Berkeley, CA: Ulysses Press, 1999.

Milne, Lorus and Margery. *Audubon Society Field Guide to North American Insects and Spiders.* New York: Alfred A. Knopf, 1986.

Perry, Ben Edward, ed. and trans. *Babrius and Phaedrus.* London: Harvard University Press, 1965.

Pickering, David. *Dictionary of Superstitions.* London: Cassell, 1995.

Saunders, Nicholas J. *Animal Spirits.* Boston: Little, Brown, 1995.

Spector, Norman B., ed. *Complete Fables of Jean de la Fontaine.* Evanston, IL: Northwestern University Press, 1988.

ON THE INTERNET

The Amateur Entomologists' Society Bug Club
    www.ex.ac.uk/bugclub/welcome.html

Bug Bios
    www.bugbios.com

Canadian Broadcasting Company Tree Crickets: An Insect Inspection
    www.cbc4kids.ca/general/the-lab/big-bang/99-02-18

Entomology Index of Internet Resources
    www.ent.iastate.edu/list/

Insects & More
    http://tqjunior.thinkquest.org/5135/insects.htm

Insects: Research/Information Sites
    http://edtech.kennesaw.edu/web/insects.html

PBS Online's Alien Empire
    www.pbs.org/wnet/nature/alienempire/

The Wonderful World of Insects
    www.earthlife.net/insects/

INDEX

79